May you come to know and love our Lord and Savior
through the love of His Blessed Mother.

To: _____

From: _____

On this Day: _____

ALL SOULS TO HEAVEN
A Catholic Family's Complete Guide to the Rosary

Written and Curated by Tom Wall
Illustrated by Martin Whitmore
Layout by Ron Tupper

Aquinas Ventures, LLC
Green Bay, Wisconsin 54305

Nihil Obstat
Reverend James P. Massart, D. Min., Ph.D.

Imprimatur
The Most Reverend David L. Ricken, DD, JCL
Bishop of Green Bay

Green Bay, Wisconsin   USA

April 13, 2016

The *Nihil Obstat* and *Imprimatur* are official declarations that a book is considered to be free of doctrinal or moral error.
It is not implied that those who have granted the *Nihil Obstat* or *Imprimatur*
agree with the contents, opinions, or statements expressed.

FIRST EDITION

OurCatholicFuture.com

ISBN: 978-0-9908950-4-6

Printed in China.

St. Louis de Montfort quotes from *The Secret of the Rosary* by St. Louis Mary de Montfort. © 1987 Montfort Publications, Bay Shore, NY. TAN Books Charlotte, NC. All rights reserved.

St. Pope John Paul II quotes from the Apostolic Letter *Rosarium Virginis Mariae* (sections 7, 25, 40, and 43) by Pope John Paul II, October 16, 2002. © Libreria Editrice Vaticana. Vatican City. All rights reserved.

St. Josemaría Escrivá quotes from *Holy Rosary* (#12), *The Furrow* (# 475), and *The Way* (# 558) by St. Josemaría Escrivá. © Fundación Studium Madrid, Spain. Scepter Publishers Strongsville, OH. All rights reserved.

Mysteries of the Rosary section from *The Rosary Handbook* by Mitch Finley. © 2007 Mitch Finley. The Word Among Us Press, Fredrick, MD. All rights reserved.

The Most Holy Rosary, History of the Rosary, St. Dominic, Promises of the Rosary, Battle of Lepanto, Fatima, and Lourdes sections from their respective Wikipedia® pages. https://en.wikipedia.org/wiki/

Feasts of the Rosary and Year of the Rosary from their respective Wikipedia® pages. https://en.wikipedia.org/wiki/

Short biographies of Bl. Bartolo Longo, St. Louis de Montfort, and Pope Pius XIII from their respective Wikipedia® pages. https://en.wikipedia.org/wiki/

In memory of...

my Uncle Tony.
He always tried to see Christ in others, and showed compassion and mercy
to the many people who saw Christ in him...staying true to his Church until the end.

Dedicated to...

all the special people in your life who always had their beads nearby.

May their love and devotion to Jesus and His Mother
continue to live in your heart for generations to come.

With Gratitude to...

my Mom.
You've dedicated your life to loving and serving our family... thanks Mom, I love you.

THE MOST HOLY ROSARY

The Rosary prayer is a repetitive, Scripture-based devotion that is prayed with rosary beads.

The Rosary is considered to be a "Christocentric" prayer because it is centered on Jesus.

Throughout the entire Rosary, we focus on our Lord Jesus Christ –
His Life, Ministry, Death, Resurrection, Ascension into Heaven, and the Sending of the Holy Spirit –
while also honoring the Blessed Virgin Mary.

The Rosary helps us recall and meditate on the important events of both Jesus and His Blessed Mother.
Praying the Rosary helps us grow closer to Jesus through our love for Mary.

Did you know?

The word Rosary comes for the Latin word *Rosarium*,
which means "Crown of Roses" or "Garland of Roses".

"Let us crown ourselves with roses of the Most Holy Rosary." – *St. Louis de Montfort*

> "In the Rosary,
> we not only *say* prayers;
> we *think* them."
>
> −Ven. Archbishop Fulton Sheen

The Rosary is a unique prayer because it engages us in various ways when we pray it. Not only do we engage spiritually with the Rosary prayer, we also engage with it physically, vocally, and mentally.

PHYSICAL: We hold the rosary and move from bead to bead.

VOCAL: We speak the prayer (either silently or out loud).

MENTAL: We think about each Mystery as we pray the five decades.

Venerable Archbishop Fulton J. Sheen
1895–1979

Some people think that praying the Rosary
can become too repetitive because we recite
the same prayers over and over again.
And, some people say they get distracted easily when praying it.

The beauty of the Rosary actually lies in the repetition of its prayers
and the freedom to meditate on the life of Jesus and Mary.
When we pray the Rosary, we're able to enter into this rhythmic
prayer and deep reflection. Each time we move our fingers
from bead to bead, we grow closer to our Blessed Mother
and her Son Jesus.

"Say the Holy Rosary. Blessed be that monotony of Hail Marys
which purifies the monotony of your sins!" – *St. Josemaría Escrivá*

Did you know?

There are numerous types of Rosaries and many of them
have a different number of beads.

A few examples are the Dominican Rosary, the Chaplet Rosary,
the Auto Rosary, the Lasso Rosary, the Missionary Rosary,
the Seraphic Rosary (Seven Joys), and the Servite Rosary (Seven Sorrows).

Most rosary beads are made of wood, glass, plastic, knotted cord, or metal.
There are even rosaries that glow in the dark!

The Rosary Ring

The Rosary Ring
is a small metal ring
that consists of one decade
of the Rosary and is often
placed on a key chain.

THE HISTORY OF THE ROSARY

The first rosary dates back to approximately the twelfth century.

It was customary for priests, monks, and other members of the clergy to pray or chant the Daily Office, consisting of the 150 Psalms from the Old Testament, also known as the Psalter of David.

They would wear 150 beads around their waists and use these strings of beads to help them count and keep track of each Psalm.

Although clergy members were formally educated, many lay people who desired to learn and practice their faith were not. Unfortunately, they weren't able to read and learn the Psalter of David.

Instead of reciting the Psalms of David within the Daily Office, they replaced the 150 Psalms with the Psalter of the Laity. This Psalter consisted of either 150 Aves (Hail Mary's) or 150 Pater Nosters (Our Father's).

"There is no devotion so generally practiced by the faithful of all classes as that of the Rosary."
– *St. Alphonsus Liguori*

ST. DOMINIC

Although there are a number of different accounts regarding how, when, and where the Rosary started, the most commonly accepted origin of the Rosary dates back to Blessed Alan de Roche's account of when Mary appeared to St. Dominic in 1214.

Tradition has it that when St. Dominic was praying for the conversion of souls in the countryside of France, Mary appeared to him. She consoled him, gave him the Rosary, and taught him how to pray it.

She instructed him to pray the Rosary and share it throughout the world in order to bring more people to her son Jesus.

THE PROMISES OF THE ROSARY

When Our Lady of the Rosary taught St. Dominic the Rosary prayer and asked him to spread the devotion, it is believed that she made 15 promises to all those who pray it faithfully.

A few of the promises of the Rosary are:

- To all those who shall recite my Rosary devoutly, I promise my special protection and very great graces.
- Those who trust themselves to me through the Rosary shall not perish.
- Those who shall recite my Rosary devoutly, meditating on its mysteries, shall not be overwhelmed by misfortune. The sinner shall be converted; the just shall grow in grace and become worthy of eternal life.
- Those who recite my Rosary shall find during their life and at their death the light of God, the fullness of His graces, and shall share in the merits of the blessed.
- Those who propagate my Rosary shall be aided by me in all their necessities.

The Battle of Lepanto

POPE ST. PIUS V

Pope Pius V, a Dominican, officially established the Catholic Church's devotion to the Rosary when he issued the papal bull (an official papal document) called *Consueverunt Romani Pontifices* in 1569. In this document he established the original 15 Mysteries and also granted indulgences for praying the Rosary.

THE BATTLE OF LEPANTO

 On October 7, 1571 the Christian European military, called the Holy League, was at war with the Islamic Turkish military. These two forces were engaged in the Battle of Lepanto on the coast of what is now the country of Greece.

During this naval battle, Pope Pius V called on all Christians throughout Europe to pray the Rosary. While everyone was praying the Rosary, the Pope petitioned Our Lady of Victory to intercede on the Holy League's behalf to help them defeat the Turkish fighters.

The Christian Holy League won the Battle of Lepanto and Pope Pius V gave credit to the intercession of Mary as the reason they won it.

To honor Mary for her protection and intercession, Pope Pius V declared October 7 as the Feast of Our Lady of Victory.

Pope St. Pius V
1504–1572

"I urge you all to recite the Rosary every day, abandoning yourselves with trust in Mary's hands."
– *Pope Benedict XVI*

Our Lady of Fatima
Feast Day: May 13

OUR LADY OF FATIMA

> ## "Pray the Rosary every day
> ## to obtain peace for the world."
>
> *– Our Lady of Fátima*

Our Lady of the Holy Rosary of Fátima appeared to three young shepherd children for the first time on May 13, 1917 in Fátima, Portugal. She continued to appear to them five more times until October 13 of the same year when the Miracle of the Sun appeared.

These three Portuguese children, Lucia Dos Santos and her younger cousins Francisco and Jacinta Marto, described Our Lady of Fatima's appearance as "brighter than the sun, shedding rays of light clearer and stronger than a crystal goblet filled with the most sparkling water and pierced by the burning rays of the sun."

Our Lady of Fatima asked the children to do three things:

1. Pray the Rosary.
2. Do penance (avoid and confess sins).
3. Honor the Immaculate Heart of Mary.

The Feast Day of Our Lady of Fátima is May 13.

"The Rosary has a peaceful effect on those who pray it." – *Pope St. John Paul II*

OUR LADY OF LOURDES

On February 11, 1856, the Virgin Mary appeared to a 14 year-old girl named Bernadette Soubirous on the mountainside of Lourdes, France for the first time when she was gathering firewood.

Bernadette told the people of her town that a beautiful young woman wearing a white gown and a blue sash with two golden roses on her feet and a golden rosary on her arm appeared to her.

Although Our Lady of Lourdes appeared to Bernadette a total of 18 times, many townspeople, and even the Church didn't believe her at first.

On each of the apparitions, Bernadette asked the woman who she was, but it wasn't until the 16th time that she answered her. It was during this apparition that she told Bernadette,

"I am the Immaculate Conception."

St. Bernadette was canonized by Pope Pius XI on December 8, 1933, the Feast of the Immaculate Conception.

The Feast of Our Lady of Lourdes is celebrated on February 11.

"O Most Holy Rosary, may your flowers bloom on the desolate flowerbeds of unbelievers and let simple and lively faith come to bloom again." – *Fr. Dolindo Ruotolo*

Our Lady of Lourdes
Feast Day: February 11

St. Bernadette
Feast Day: April 16

DEVOTION TO THE ROSARY

"The greatest method of praying is to pray the Rosary."

—*St. Francis de Sales*

St. Francis de Sales
1567–1622

"Recite your Rosary with faith, with humility, with confidence, and with perseverance." - *St. Louis de Montfort*

"Do you want to love Our Lady?
Well, then, get to know her.
How?
By praying her Rosary."

– *St. Josemaría Escrivá*

**St. Josemaría Escrivá
1902-1975**

"Do you pray the Rosary every day?" – Pope Francis

BLESSED BARTOLO LONGO

"Sweet queen of my heart, kindly accept the prayer I address to you:
that your love may spread in my heart and in the hearts of all those
who honor you by reciting the blessed rosary."

– Bl. Bartolo Longo

Bartolo Longo grew up in a devout Catholic family in Italy.
When he was older, he moved away to study law and completely
rejected God and the Catholic Church. He eventually became a lawyer
and began suffering from anxiety and depression. During this difficult time,
Bartolo met a Dominican priest who taught him the Catholic faith.

After much studying and praying, Bartolo came back to the Church
and became a Third Order Dominican. He devoted the rest of his life
to serving others while spreading his devotion to the Most Holy Rosary.

Bartolo Longo received the title of "Blessed" when he was beatified
during the Month of the Rosary on October 26, 1980 by Pope John Paul II.
Over twenty years later, Pope John Paul II mentioned Longo
in his Apostolic Letter *Rosarium Virginis Mariae*, referring to him as
the "Apostle of the Rosary".

Bl. Bartolo Longo
1841-1926

SAINT LOUIS DE MONTFORT

> "The Rosary is a priceless treasure inspired by God."
> – *St. Louis De Montfort*

St. Louis de Montfort was ordained a priest in France in 1700.

He received the title of Apostolic Missionary from Pope Clement XI and started a group of missionaries called the Company of Mary in 1705. As a writer and missionary preacher, he walked across all of France from one mission to another, sharing his love for Jesus through Mary and preaching the importance of praying the Rosary everywhere he went.

In his book *The Secret of the Rosary* he writes in depth about this treasured devotion and its many blessings. In the book *True Devotion to Mary* he focuses on the role of the Virgin Mary as a Mediatrix to her Son Jesus and consecration "to Jesus through Mary".

Louis de Montfort was beatified in 1888 by Pope Leo XIII and canonized by Pope Pius XII in 1947. We celebrate the feast day of St. Louis de Montfort on April 28.

St. Louis de Montfort
1673-1716

Did you know?

The word 'Mediatrix' refers to how
the Blessed Virgin Mary can intercede
on behalf of her Son Jesus.

To Jesus through Mary.

Although Jesus is the one true Mediator
between us and God, we can call upon Mary's motherly love
to bring us closer to her Son.

POPE LEO XIII

"The Rosary is the most excellent form of prayer and the most efficacious means of attaining eternal life. It is the remedy for all our evils, the root of all our blessings. There is no more excellent way of praying."

– Pope Leo XIII

Pope Leo XIII had a special devotion to Jesus through our Lord's Blessed Mother. As a result, he was the first pope to fully embrace Mary as Mediatrix.

Known as the "Rosary Pope", Pope Leo XIII was a strong advocate of praying and promoting the Rosary as a public devotion in parishes around the world.

During his 25-year papacy, he wrote 11 Encyclicals about the Rosary. Pope Leo XIII also wrote the Prayer to St. Michael the Archangel.

Along with being devoted to spreading his love for the Blessed Mother, Pope Leo XIII also focused on strengthening the Catholic Church within the modern world. He used his diplomatic skills to improve relations with world leaders and to influence economic conditions for the working class. As Pontiff, Pope Leo XIII also encouraged the study of natural science, believing that science and religion can exist together.

Pope Leo XIII
1810–1903

FEASTS OF THE ROSARY

THE MONTH OF THE ROSARY

While the entire month of October is dedicated to the Most Holy Rosary, the Feast of Our Lady of the Rosary is celebrated on October 7.

THE FEAST OF OUR LADY OF THE ROSARY

The Feast of Our Lady of the Rosary has seen a number changes since it was first established over 400 years ago.

This feast day was originally established as the 'Feast of Our Lady of Victory' by Pope Pius V in 1571 to celebrate and remember Mary's intercession during the Battle of Lepanto. Two years after that battle, Pope Gregory XIII changed the name of the feast day from the 'Feast of Our Lady of Victory' to the 'Feast of the Holy Rosary'.

In 1716 Pope Clement XI added the feast day to the General Roman Calendar so that the entire Church would celebrate the Feast of the Holy Rosary on the first Sunday of October.

Nearly 200 years later, in 1913, Pope Pius X moved the feast day from the first Sunday of October back to October 7. In 1960, Pope John XXIII changed the name from the 'Feast of the Holy Rosary' to the 'Feast of Our Lady of the Rosary'.

YEAR OF THE ROSARY

"Confidently take up the Rosary once again.
Rediscover the Rosary in the light of Scripture,
in harmony with the Liturgy,
and in the context of your daily lives."

– *Pope St. John Paul II*

In October of 2002 Pope John Paul II published his Apostolic Letter called *Rosarium Virginis Mariae* and declared the time between October 2002 and October 2003 as the 'Year of the Rosary'.

In this Apostolic Letter, Pope John Paul II proposed the addition of a fourth set of Mysteries called the Luminous Mysteries.

Also known as the Mysteries of Light, this new set of five Mysteries focuses on the public ministries of Jesus and are meditated upon on Thursdays.

**Pope St. John Paul II
1920-2005**

PRAYING THE ROSARY

The Rosary can be prayed silently by yourself. It can also be prayed out loud with other people.

Whether praying alone or in a group, many people choose to pray the Rosary for a special intention. Sometimes we may choose to pray for our own needs, but many times we pray for the needs of others.

Praying the Rosary as a group is a common tradition in many Catholic parishes and households. When prayed as a group, the Rosary is said out loud and most of the prayers are recited in two parts.

Typically one person in the group leads the others by announcing each Mystery and reciting the first part of each prayer. The rest of the group recites the second part of the prayer together.

The second part of the Our Father begins with:
"Give us this day our daily bread..."

The second part of the Hail Mary begins with:
"Holy Mary, Mother of God..."

The second part of the Glory Be begins with:
"As it was in the beginning..."

"The Rosary is the most beautiful
and the most rich in graces of all prayers;
it is the prayer that touches most
the Heart of the Mother of God...
and if you wish peace to reign in your homes,
recite the family Rosary."

– *Pope St. Pius X*

Pope St. Pius X
1835-1914

"It would be impossible to name all the many saints who discovered in the Rosary
a genuine path to growth in holiness." - *Pope St. John Paul II*

THE ROSARY AT CHURCH AND SCHOOL

In many parishes, it is customary to pray the Rosary as a group before or after Mass. Numerous parishes have even started the children's Rosary.
The Rosary is also traditionally prayed at wake services.

At many Catholic schools, teachers and students pray one decade of the Rosary on each day of the week. Between Monday and Friday,
they end up praying all five decades of the Rosary!

THE ROSARY AT HOME

Some families have a designated day of the week or time of day when they pray the Rosary together. And some families also pray the Rosary when they're in the car during long drives.

In his Encyclical *Ingruentium Malorum*,
Pope Pius XII encouraged families
to pray the Rosary together.

Pope Pius XII
1876-1958

"The family that prays together, stays together." – *Servant of God Fr. Patrick Peyton*

The Family Rosary

THE DOMINICAN ROSARY

The most popular and traditional Rosary is called the Dominican Rosary.

The traditional Dominican Rosary
has a total of 59 beads
and consists of opening prayers,
five decades, and closing prayers.

The traditional Dominican Rosary is made up of
the following prayers and meditations:

53 Hail Mary's
6 Our Father's
6 Glory Be's
5 Mysteries
5 Fatima Prayers (optional)
2 Signs of the Cross
1 Apostles' Creed
1 Hail, Holy Queen
1 Rosary Prayer

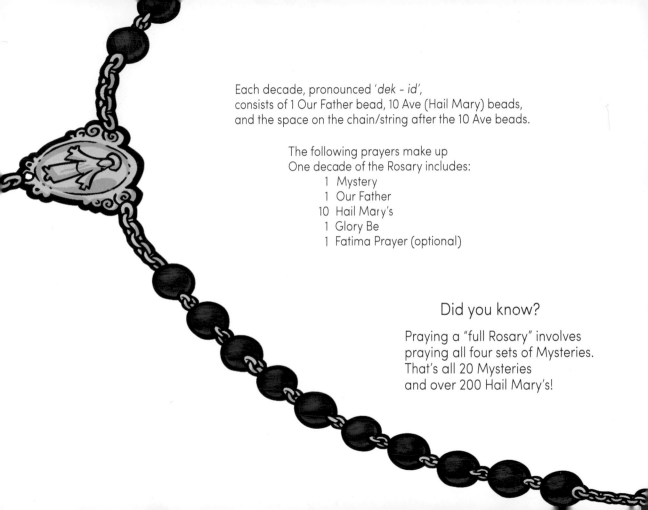

Each decade, pronounced 'dek - id',
consists of 1 Our Father bead, 10 Ave (Hail Mary) beads,
and the space on the chain/string after the 10 Ave beads.

The following prayers make up
One decade of the Rosary includes:
    1 Mystery
    1 Our Father
  10 Hail Mary's
    1 Glory Be
    1 Fatima Prayer (optional)

Did you know?

Praying a "full Rosary" involves
praying all four sets of Mysteries.
That's all 20 Mysteries
and over 200 Hail Mary's!

THE SIGN OF THE CROSS

We begin and end the Rosary prayer by holding the Cross and reciting the Sign of the Cross.

This vocal and physical prayer calls upon the Holy Trinity as we use our right hand to make the Sign of the Cross on our forehead, chest, and left and right shoulders.

Sign of the Cross

In the name of the Father, and of the Son, and of the Holy Spirit. Amen.

THE APOSTLES' CREED

The Apostles' Creed dates back over 1,600 years ago to the 4th century. It is believed that all Twelve Apostles contributed to writing the Apostles' Creed under the inspiration of the Holy Spirit.

The Apostles' Creed is the second prayer of the Rosary that we pray while still holding the Cross.

Apostles' Creed

I believe in God,
the Father almighty,
Creator of heaven and earth,
and in Jesus Christ, his only Son, our Lord,
who was conceived by the Holy Spirit,
born of the Virgin Mary,
suffered under Pontius Pilate,
was crucified, died and was buried;
he descended into hell;
on the third day he rose again from the dead;
he ascended into heaven,
and is seated at the right hand of God the Father almighty;
from there he will come to judge the living and the dead.
I believe in the Holy Spirit,
the holy catholic Church,
the communion of saints,
the forgiveness of sins,
the resurrection of the body,
and life everlasting.
Amen.

THE LORD'S PRAYER

The Lord's Prayer, also known as The Our Father, comes directly from the Bible in Matthew 6: 9-13.

In the gospel of Matthew, we read that Jesus walked throughout Galilee where He invited His Twelve Apostles to follow Him. Along the way, He stopped to teach and preach the Good News of the Kingdom of God. As He went from town to town, Jesus also cured the sick. As the news spread about the miracles that Jesus was performing, crowds began to form and they followed Him everywhere He went.

When Jesus noticed all of the people following Him, he went up the side of the mountain and preached to them. It was here that Jesus taught His disciples how to pray.

Our Father

Our Father, who art in Heaven,
hallowed be Thy name;
Thy kingdom come;
Thy will be done
on earth as it is in Heaven.

Give us this day our daily bread
and forgive us our trespasses
as we forgive those
who trespass against us;
and lead us not into temptation,
but deliver us from evil. Amen.

THE HAIL MARY

The Hail Mary, or the *Ave Maria* in Latin, is the Rosary's central prayer
and is prayed on each of the 53 Ave (Hail Mary) beads in the traditional Rosary.

Although it is one of the most popular Marian prayers,
the Hail Mary actually focuses on our Lord Jesus and our Blessed Mother.

Hail Mary

Hail Mary, full of grace,
the Lord is with thee;

Blessed art thou among women,
and blessed is the fruit of thy womb, Jesus.

Holy Mary, Mother of God,
pray for us sinners,
now and at the hour of our death. Amen.

Because we repeat the Hail Mary so many times when we pray the Rosary,
it's not only important that we know the words of the prayer,
it's also critical that we know what the words truly mean!

The Hail Mary consists of three parts.
The first two parts include words of admiration, and the third part includes words of honor and petition.

In the first part, we pay respect to Mary by repeating the Angel Gabriel's greeting to her from Luke 1:28.
When God's messenger Gabriel appeared to Mary, he told her that God had chosen her to be the Mother of Jesus.

Hail Mary, full of grace,
the Lord is with thee;

After Mary said yes to God's plan to give birth to Jesus, she went to visit her pregnant cousin Elizabeth.
We continue revering our Blessed Mother in the second part by repeating the words Elizabeth proclaimed
when Mary entered her house, found in Luke 1:42. At the center of the Hail Mary, we stop to worship our Lord Jesus.

Blessed art thou among women,
and blessed is the fruit of thy womb, Jesus.

In the third part, we invoke Mary's intercession as Jesus' Mother and ask her to pray for us.

Holy Mary, Mother of God,
pray for us sinners,
now and at the hour of our death. Amen.

We conclude by acknowledging we don't always do what's right and by asking our Blessed Mother to pray for us –
both today and during the final moments of our life.

THE GLORY BE

The Glory Be, or the Doxology, is prayed immediately after the 10 Hail Mary's of each decade.

Glory Be

Glory be to the Father,
and to the Son,
and the Holy Spirit;
as it was in the beginning,
is now,
and ever shall be,
world without end. Amen.

The Glory Be is considered a Trinitarian prayer because it focuses on the Holy Trinity.

The Holy Trinity is one God in three persons –

$$1 + 1 + 1 = 1$$

God the Father, Jesus the Son, and the Holy Spirit.

The Holy Trinity

THE FATIMA PRAYER

The Fatima Prayer, also known as the Decade prayer, is a form of the Jesus Prayer.

This is the prayer that Our Lady of Fatima taught to the three shepherd children when she appeared to them in 1917.

Because the Fatima Prayer is not part of the original Dominican Rosary,
it is an optional prayer that is said after the Glory Be at the end of each Decade.

Fatima Prayer

O my Jesus, forgive us our sins,
save us from the fires of hell,
lead all souls to Heaven,
especially those in most need of Your Mercy.

THE HAIL, HOLY QUEEN

The Hail, Holy Queen, or the *Salve Regina* in Latin, is one of the final prayers of the Rosary. It is prayed after completing all five decades.

Hail, Holy Queen
(Salve Regina)

Hail, Holy Queen, Mother of Mercy,
our life, our sweetness and our hope.
To thee do we cry,
Poor banished children of Eve;
To thee do we send up our sighs,
mourning and weeping in this valley of tears.
Turn then, most gracious advocate,
Thine eyes of mercy toward us;
And after this our exile,
Show unto us the blessed fruit of thy womb, Jesus.
O clement, O loving, O sweet Virgin Mary.

V. Pray for us, O holy Mother of God,
R. that we may be made worthy of the promises of Christ.

The Rosary Prayer is traditionally the final prayer of the Rosary.

Rosary Prayer

O God, whose Only Begotten Son,
by his Life, Death, and Resurrection,
has purchased for us the rewards of eternal life.
Grant, we beseech thee,
that while meditating on these mysteries
of the Most Holy Rosary of the Blessed Virgin Mary,
we may imitate what they contain
and obtain what they promise,
through the same Christ our Lord. Amen.

THE MYSTERIES OF THE ROSARY

The Mysteries of the Rosary are the important events in the lives of Jesus and Mary that are meditated upon while praying each decade of the Rosary.

Until 2002, there were three sets of Mysteries. The original three sets of Mysteries are the Joyful, the Glorious, and the Sorrowful. In 2002, Pope John Paul II suggested the addition of a fourth set of Mysteries called the Luminous.

Each of the four sets contain five Mysteries... adding up to twenty Mysteries in all.
All but two of the twenty Mysteries come directly from the Bible.

Associated with every Mystery is a "Fruit of the Rosary". Each of these "fruits" is a virtue, or a benefit, that we receive from meditating upon the Mystery.

Glorious
Mysteries

Joyful
Mysteries

Sorrowful
Mysteries

Luminous
Mysteries

Did you know?

The Mysteries of the Rosary are not called "Mysteries" because they are unknown events that need to be solved.
They're called "Mysteries" because they are works of God in the lives of Jesus and Mary
and it can be difficult to understand their full meaning.

During <u>ORDINARY TIME</u>:

Pray and mediate on the following mysteries on the following days...

MONDAY	TUESDAY	WEDNESDAY	THURSDAY	FRIDAY	SATURDAY	SUNDAY
Joyful Mysteries	Sorrowful Mysteries	Glorious Mysteries	Luminous Mysteries	Sorrowful Mysteries	Joyful Mysteries	Glorious Mysteries

During <u>the SEASON OF ADVENT</u>.

Follow the calendar for ORDINARY TIME, except...
CHANGE Sunday to the Joyful Mysteries.

During <u>the SEASON OF LENT</u>:

Follow the calendar for ORDINARY TIME, except...
CHANGE Monday through Saturday to the Sorrowful Mysteries (Sunday stays the same).

THE GLORIOUS MYSTERIES

The Glorious Mysteries help us recall events that focus on our Lord's Resurrection and His saving Grace. They also help us remember important events that focus on our Blessed Mother.

We meditate on the Glorious Mysteries when we pray the Rosary on Wednesdays and Sundays.

1st Mystery	2nd Mystery	3rd Mystery	4th Mystery	5th Mystery

The Resurrection *Luke 24:1–12*	**The Ascension** *Luke 24:50–51*	**The Descent of the Holy Spirit** *Acts 2:1–4*	**The Assumption of Mary**	**The Coronation of the Virgin Mary**
Fruit: Faith	Fruit: Hope	Fruit: Love of God	Fruit: Grace of a Happy Death	Fruit: Trust in Mary's Intercession

THE JOYFUL MYSTERIES

The Joyful Mysteries help us recall events that focus on our Lord's Incarnation and early childhood. We meditate on the Joyful Mysteries when praying the Rosary on Mondays and Saturdays.

On Sundays during the season of Advent, some people choose to meditate on the Joyful Mysteries instead of the usual Glorious Mysteries.

1st Mystery

The Annunciation
Luke 1:26-38

Fruit: Humility

2nd Mystery

The Visitation
Luke 1:40-56

Fruit: Love of Neighbor

3rd Mystery

The Nativity
Luke 2:6-20

Fruit: Poverty

4th Mystery

The Presentation of Jesus at the Temple
Luke 2:21-39

Fruit: Obedience

5th Mystery

The Finding of Jesus in the Temple
Luke 2:41-51

Fruit: Joy in Finding Jesus

THE SORROWFUL MYSTERIES

The Sorrowful Mysteries help us recall events that focus on our Lord's Suffering and Death during His Passion. We meditate on the Sorrowful Mysteries when praying the Rosary on Tuesdays and Fridays.

During the season of Lent, you may choose to meditate on the Sorrowful Mysteries on every day you pray the Rosary, except on Sunday. On Sundays during Lent, we meditate on the Glorious Mysteries.

1st Mystery	2nd Mystery	3rd Mystery	4th Mystery	5th Mystery
The Agony in the Garden *Matthew 26:36–46*	**The Scourging at the Pillar** *Matthew 27:26*	**The Crowning with Thorns** *Matthew 27:29*	**The Carrying of the Cross** *John 19:17*	**The Crucifixion** *Luke 23:33–46*
Fruit: Sorrow for Sin	Fruit: Purity	Fruit: Courage	Fruit: Patience	Fruit: Perseverance

THE LUMINOUS MYSTERIES

The Luminous Mysteries, also called the Mysteries of Light, help us recall events that focus on our Lord's public Ministry.

We meditate on the Luminous Mysteries when praying the Rosary on Thursdays.

| 1st Mystery | 2nd Mystery | 3rd Mystery | 4th Mystery | 5th Mystery |

The Baptism of Jesus in the Jordan
Matthew 3:13-17
Mark 1:9-11
Luke 3:21-22

Fruit: Openness to the Holy Spirit

The Wedding at Cana
John 2:1-11

Fruit: To Jesus through Mary

The Proclamation of the Kingdom of God
Matthew 10:7-8

Fruit: Repentance and Trust in God

The Transfiguration
Matthew 17:1-9
Mark 9:2-10
Luke 9:28-36

Fruit: Desire for Holiness

The Institution of the Eucharist
Matthew 26:26-29
Mark 14:22-25
Luke 22:19-20

Fruit: Adoration

HOW TO PRAY THE ROSARY

1. Begin by holding the Crucifix — recite the *Sign of the Cross* and the *Apostles' Creed*.

2. Pray the *Our Father*.

3. Pray three *Hail Marys* (for an increase in Faith, Hope, and Charity).

4. Pray the *Glory Be* and the optional *Fatima Prayer* in the space between the tenth *Ave* bead and the *Our Father* bead that follows.

5. Announce and meditate upon the first Mystery, then pray the *Our Father*.

6. Pray ten *Hail Marys* on the ten *Ave (Hail Mary)* beads.

7. Pray the *Glory Be* and the optional *Fatima Prayer*.

8. On the *Our Father* bead, before each of the remaining four decades, announce and meditate upon the next Mystery, and then pray the *Our Father*.

9. During each of the following four decades, pray ten *Hail Marys*, the *Glory Be*, and the optional *Fatima Prayer*.

10. After praying all five decades, pray the *Hail, Holy Queen*, the optional *Rosary Prayer*, and conclude by reciting the *Sign of the Cross*.

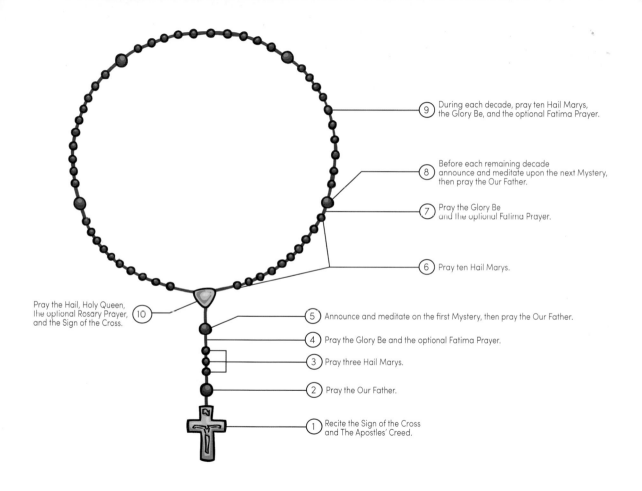

During each decade, pray ten Hail Marys, the Glory Be, and the optional Fatima Prayer.

Before each remaining decade announce and meditate upon the next Mystery, then pray the Our Father.

Pray the Glory Be and the optional Fatima Prayer.

Pray ten Hail Marys.

Pray the Hail, Holy Queen, the optional Rosary Prayer, and the Sign of the Cross.

Announce and meditate on the first Mystery, then pray the Our Father.

Pray the Glory Be and the optional Fatima Prayer.

Pray three Hail Marys.

Pray the Our Father.

Recite the Sign of the Cross and The Apostles' Creed.

INTRODUCTORY PRAYERS

The Sign of the Cross

In the name of the Father, and of the Son, and of the Holy Spirit. Amen.

The Apostles' Creed

I believe in God, the Father almighty,
Creator of heaven and earth,
and in Jesus Christ, his only Son, our Lord,
who was conceived by the Holy Spirit,
born of the Virgin Mary,
suffered under Pontius Pilate,
was crucified, died and was buried;
he descended into hell;
on the third day he rose again from the dead;
he ascended into heaven,
and is seated at the right hand of God the Father almighty;
from there he will come to judge the living and the dead.
I believe in the Holy Spirit, the holy catholic Church,
the communion of saints, the forgiveness of sins,
the resurrection of the body, and life everlasting.
Amen.

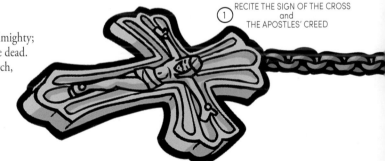

1 RECITE THE SIGN OF THE CROSS
and
THE APOSTLES' CREED

The Our Father

Our Father, who art in Heaven,
hallowed be Thy name;
Thy kingdom come;
Thy will be done
on earth as it is in Heaven.

Give us this day our daily bread
and forgive us our trespasses
as we forgive those who trespass against us;
and lead us not into temptation,
but deliver us from evil.
Amen.

The Hail Mary

Hail Mary, full of grace,
the Lord is with thee;

Blessed art thou among women,
and blessed is the fruit of thy womb, Jesus.

Holy Mary, Mother of God,
pray for us sinners,
now and at the hour of our death.
Amen.

The Glory Be

Glory be to the Father,
and tothe Son,
and the Holy Spirit;
as it was in the beginning,
is now,
and ever shall be,
world without end.
Amen.

The Fatima Prayer

O my Jesus, forgive us our sins, save us from the fires of hell,
lead all souls to Heaven, especially those in most need of Your Mercy.

② PRAY ONE OUR FATHER

③ For Faith, Hope, and Charity...
PRAY THREE HAIL MARYS

④ PRAY THE GLORY BE

⑤ PRAY THE FATIMA PRAYER

THE 1ˢᵗ GLORIOUS MYSTERY:
THE RESURRECTION OF JESUS

Fruit of the Mystery: **Faith**

Three days after Jesus died on the Cross, He rose from the dead and the tomb that His body was placed in was empty.

THE 1ˢᵗ JOYFUL MYSTERY:
THE ANNUNCIATION

Fruit of the Mystery: **Humilty**

God sent the Angel Gabriel to the town of Nazareth to tell the Virgin Mary, the fiancé of Joseph, that God chose her to be the Mother of Jesus.

1. ANNOUNCE & MEDITATE ON THE 1ˢᵗ MYSTERY

2. PRAY ONE OUR FATHER

3. PRAY TEN HAIL MARYS

THE 1st SORROWFUL MYSTERY:
THE AGONY IN THE GARDEN

Fruit of the Mystery: **Sorrow for Sin**

Before Jesus was arrested in the Garden of Gethsemane, He asked His Apostles to stay near Him while He prayed – but they fell asleep.

THE 1st LUMINOUS MYSTERY:
THE BAPTISM OF JESUS IN THE JORDAN

Fruit of the Mystery: **Openness to the Holy Spirit**

When Jesus was baptized by John the Baptist in the Jordan River, Heaven opened up and the Holy Spirit descended upon Him.

4 PRAY THE GLORY BE

5 PRAY THE FATIMA PRAYER

THE 2ⁿᵈ GLORIOUS MYSTERY:
THE ASCENSION OF JESUS

Fruit of the Mystery: **Hope**

After Jesus appeared to His Apostles to comfort them and send them out into the world, He ascended into Heaven and was seated at the right hand of God.

THE 2ⁿᵈ JOYFUL MYSTERY:
THE VISITATION

Fruit of the Mystery: **Love of Neighbor**

When Mary went to visit her cousin Elizabeth, the baby inside Elizabeth's womb leapt with joy because the baby knew he was in the presence of the Lord Jesus.

① ANNOUNCE & MEDITATE ON THE 2ⁿᵈ MYSTERY

② PRAY ONE OUR FATHER

③ PRAY TEN HAIL MARYS

THE 2nd SORROWFUL MYSTERY:
THE SCOURIGING AT THE PILLAR

Fruit of the Mystery: **Purity**

After the Roman soldiers arrested Jesus, they took Him into the City of Jerusalem and whipped and tortured Him.

THE 2nd LUMINOUS MYSTERY:
THE WEDDING AT CANA

Fruit of the Mystery: **To Jesus through Mary**

Jesus performed His first public miracle at the Wedding of Cana when he turned water into the finest wine.

4 PRAY THE GLORY BE

5 PRAY THE FATIMA PRAYER

SUNDAY & WEDNESDAY

THE 3ʳᵈ GLORIOUS MYSTERY
THE DESCENT OF THE HOLY SPIRIT

Fruit of the Mystery: **Love of God**

Fifty days after Jesus rose from the dead, the Holy Spirit descended upon the Apostles and Mary who were together in the Upper Room.

MONDAY & SATURDAY

THE 3ʳᵈ JOYFUL MYSTERY
THE NATIVITY

Fruit of the Mystery: **Poverty**

There was no room at the inn, so Mary and Joseph had to go to a stable with farm animals to give birth to the baby Jesus.

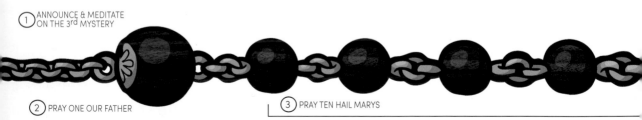

1. ANNOUNCE & MEDITATE ON THE 3ʳᵈ MYSTERY

2. PRAY ONE OUR FATHER

3. PRAY TEN HAIL MARYS

THE 3rd SORROWFUL MYSTERY:
THE CROWNING WITH THORNS

Fruit of the Mystery: **Courage**

The soldiers stripped Jesus of His clothes and placed a purple cloak on His shoulders, put a crown of thorns on His head, and ridiculed Him.

THE 3rd LUMINOUS MYSTERY:
THE PROCLAMATION OF THE KINGDOM OF GOD

Fruit of the Mystery: **Repentance and Trust in God**

As Jesus went from town to town healing the sick and preaching to His followers, He taught His Twelve Apostles to spread the Good News.

④ PRAY THE GLORY BE

⑤ PRAY THE FATIMA PRAYER

THE 4th GLORIOUS MYSTERY:
THE ASSUMPTION OF MARY

Fruit of the Mystery: **Grace of a Happy Death**

At the end of Mary's earthly life, her whole body and soul were assumed directly into Heaven by our Lord.

THE 4th JOYFUL MYSTERY:
THE PRESENTATION OF JESUS AT THE TEMPLE

Fruit of the Mystery: **Obedience**

Forty days after Jesus was born, the Holy Family went to the Temple in Jerusalem so that Simeon could meet the newborn Jesus.

1. ANNOUNCE & MEDITATE ON THE 4th MYSTERY

2. PRAY ONE OUR FATHER

3. PRAY TEN HAIL MARYS

THE 4ᵗʰ SORROWFUL MYSTERY:
THE CARRYING OF THE CROSS

Fruit of the Mystery: **Patience**

Jesus was forced to carry His Cross along the dusty roads on the way up to Mount Calvary.

THE 4ᵗʰ LUMINOUS MYSTERY:
THE TRANSFIGURATION

Fruit of the Mystery: **Desire for Holiness**

When Jesus went to Mount Tabor to pray with three of His Apostles, His face and clothes began to shine brightly and Moses and Elijah appeared to them.

4 PRAY THE
GLORY BE

5 PRAY THE
FATIMA PRAYER

THE 5th GLORIOUS MYSTERY:
THE CORONATION OF THE VIRGIN

Fruit of the Mystery: **Trust in Mary's Intercession**

Mary, the Mother of God, was crowned the Queen of Heaven by Jesus and God with the help of the Holy Spirit.

THE 5th JOYFUL MYSTERY:
THE FINDING OF JESUS IN THE TEMPLE

Fruit of the Mystery: **Joy in Finding Jesus**

After Mary and Joseph accidentally lost Jesus at the Temple when He was a young child, they eventually found Him preaching to the elders.

① ANNOUNCE & MEDITATE ON THE 5th MYSTERY

② PRAY ONE OUR FATHER

③ PRAY TEN HAIL MARYS

THE 5ᵗʰ SORROWFUL MYSTERY:
THE CRUCIFIXION

THE 5ᵗʰ LUMINOUS MYSTERY:
THE INSTITUTION OF THE EUCHARIST

Fruit of the Mystery: **Perseverance**

When Jesus was nailed to the Cross at noon on Good Friday, the skies turned dark until He died three hours later.

Fruit of the Mystery: **Adoration**

At the Last Supper, Jesus gathered in the Upper Room with His Twelve Apostles and celebrated the first Sacrifice of the Mass.

4 PRAY THE GLORY BE

5 PRAY THE FATIMA PRAYER

CONCLUDING PRAYERS

The Hail, Holy Queen

Hail, Holy Queen, Mother of mercy,
our life, our sweetness and our hope.
To thee do we cry, poor banished children of Eve;
to thee do we send up our sighs,
mourning and weeping in this valley of tears.
Turn then, most gracious Advocate,
thine eyes of mercy toward us,
and after this our exile,
show unto us the blessed fruit of thy womb, Jesus,
O clement, O loving, O sweet Virgin Mary!

V. Pray for us, O holy Mother of God.
R. That we may be made worthy of the promises of Christ. Amen.

The Rosary Prayer

Let us Pray:
O God, whose only begotten Son,
by his life, death, and resurrection,
has purchased for us the rewards of eternal life,
grant, we beseech thee,
that while meditating on these mysteries
of the most Holy Rosary of the Blessed Virgin Mary,
we may imitate what they contain
and obtain what they promise,
through the same Christ our Lord. Amen.

① PRAY THE HAIL, HOLY QUEEN

② PRAY THE ROSARY PRAYER

ADDITIONAL PRAYERS

After praying the Rosary, it is also customary to add a few more prayers before finishing completely.

Some of the most common prayers that many people like to add at the end of praying the Rosary are...

- Prayers for the Holy Father and his Intentions
- The Litany of Loreto
- The Memorare
- Prayer to St. Michael the Archangel

PRAYERS FOR THE HOLY FATHER AND HIS INTENTIONS

For the Holy Father and his Intentions...

- One Our Father
- One Hail Mary
- One Glory Be

**Pope Francis
1936 -**

Litany of Loreto

V. Lord have mercy on us.
R. Christ have mercy on us.
V. Lord have mercy on us, Christ hear us.
R. Christ graciously hear us.

God the Father of heaven, **have mercy on us.**
God the Son, Redeemer of the world, **have mercy on us.**
God the Holy Spirit, **have mercy on us.**
Holy Trinity, one God, **have mercy on us.**

Holy Mary, pray for us.
Holy Mother of God, **pray for us.**
Holy Virgin of Virgins, **pray for us.**
Mother of Christ, **pray for us.**
Mother of divine grace, **pray for us.**
Mother most pure, **pray for us.**
Mother most chaste, **pray for us.**
Mother inviolate, **pray for us.**
Mother undefiled, **pray for us.**
Mother most amiable, **pray for us.**
Mother most admirable, **pray for us.**
Mother of good Counsel, **pray for us.**
Mother of our Creator, **pray for us.**
Mother of our Savior, **pray for us.**

Virgin most prudent, **pray for us.**
Virgin most venerable, **pray for us.**
Virgin most renowned, **pray for us.**
Virgin most powerful, **pray for us.**
Virgin most merciful, **pray for us.**
Virgin most faithful, **pray for us.**
Mirror of justice, **pray for us.**
Seat of wisdom, **pray for us.**
Cause of our joy, **pray for us.**
Spiritual vessel, **pray for us.**
Vessel of honor, **pray for us.**
Singular vessel of devotion, **pray for us.**
Mystical rose, **pray for us.**
Tower of David, **pray for us.**
Tower of ivory, **pray for us.**
House of gold, **pray for us.**
Ark of the covenant, **pray for us.**
Gate of heaven, **pray for us.**
Morning star, **pray for us.**
Health of the sick, **pray for us.**
Refuge of sinners, **pray for us.**
Comforter of the afflicted, **pray for us.**
Help of Christians, **pray for us.**

Litany of Loreto (cont.)

Queen of Angels, **pray for us.**
Queen of Patriarchs, **pray for us.**
Queen of Prophets, **pray for us.**
Queen of Apostles, **pray for us.**
Queen of Martyrs, **pray for us.**
Queen of Confessors, **pray for us.**
Queen of Virgins, **pray for us.**
Queen of all Saints, **pray for us.**
Queen conceived without original sin, **pray for us.**
Queen assumed into heaven, **pray for us.**
Queen of the most holy Rosary, **pray for us.**
Queen of families, **pray for us.**
Queen of peace, **pray for us.**

V. Lamb of God, Who takest away the sins of the world,
R. Spare us, O Lord.
V. Lamb of God, Who takest away the sins of the world,
R. Graciously hear us, O Lord.
V. Lamb of God, Who takest away the sins of the world,
R. Have mercy on us.

V. Pray for us, O holy Mother of God.
**R. That we may be made worthy
of the promises of Christ.**

Let us pray. Grant, we beseech Thee,
O Lord God, that we thy servants may enjoy
perpetual health of mind and body,
and by the glorious intercession of blessed Mary,
ever Virgin, may we be freed from present sorrow,
and rejoice in eternal happiness.
Through Christ our Lord.
R. Amen.

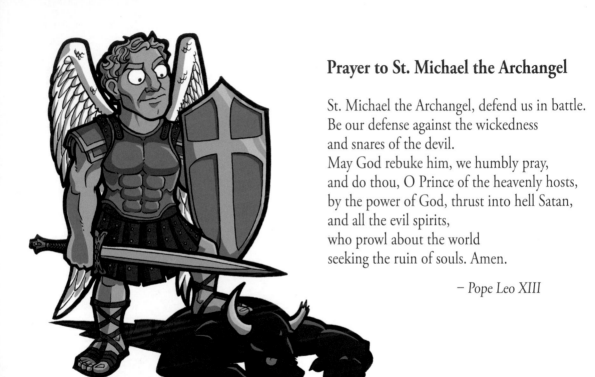

Prayer to St. Michael the Archangel

St. Michael the Archangel, defend us in battle.
Be our defense against the wickedness
and snares of the devil.
May God rebuke him, we humbly pray,
and do thou, O Prince of the heavenly hosts,
by the power of God, thrust into hell Satan,
and all the evil spirits,
who prowl about the world
seeking the ruin of souls. Amen.

– Pope Leo XIII

"Love the Madonna and pray the Rosary, for her Rosary is the weapon against the evils of the world today."
- St. Padre Pio

The Memorare

Remember, O most gracious Virgin Mary,
that never was it known that anyone
who fled to your protection,
implored your help, or sought your intercession,
was left unaided.

Inspired by this confidence, I fly unto you,
O Virgin of virgins, my Mother.
To you I come; before you I stand sinful and sorrowful.

O Mother of the Word Incarnate!
Despise not my petitions,
but in your mercy hear and answer me. Amen.

"To pray the Rosary is to hand over our burdens to the merciful hearts of Christ and His Mother."
- Pope St. John Paul II

TRADITIONAL MARIAN HYMNS

Immaculate Mary
(Lourdes Hymn)

Immaculate Mary, your praises we sing.
You reign now in heaven with Jesus our King.
Ave, Ave, Ave Maria!
Ave, Ave Maria!

In heaven the blessed your glory proclaim;
On earth we your children invoke your sweet name.
Ave, Ave, Ave Maria!
Ave, Ave Maria!

We pray for our Mother, the Church upon earth,
And bless, Holy Mary, the land of our birth.
Ave, Ave, Ave Maria!
Ave, Ave Maria!

– Lyrics attributed to Fr. Abbe Gaignet, set to a traditional French tune

Hail, Holy Queen, Enthroned Above
(Salve Regina)

Hail, holy Queen enthroned above, O Maria.
Hail, Queen of mercy and of love, O Maria.
Triumph, all ye cherubim, Sing with us, ye seraphim,
Heaven and earth resound the hymn:
Salve, salve, salve Regina!

Our life, our sweetness, here below, O Maria!
Our hope in sorrow and in woe, O Maria!
Triumph, all ye cherubim, Sing with us, ye seraphim,
Heaven and earth resound the hymn:
Salve, salve, salve Regina!

And when our last breath leaves us, O Maria
Show us thy son Christ Jesus, O Maria!
Triumph, all ye cherubim, Sing with us, ye seraphim,
Heaven and earth resound the hymn:
Salve, salve, salve Regina!

– *Traditional Hymn translated from the Salve Regina Coelitum*